P9-DTP-136

JUAN RODRIGUEZ CABRILLO

BY JOHN BANKSTON

P.O. Box 196
Hockessin, Delaware 19707

OTHER TITLES IN THE SERIES

Álvar Núñez Cabeza de Vaca

Américo Paredes

Antonio López de Santa Anna

Bernardo de Gálvez

Cesar Chavez

Diego Rivera

Dolores Huerta

Francisco Vásquez de Coronado

Fray Juan Crespí

Gaspar de Portolá

Hernando de Soto

Jovita Idar

Juan Bautista de Anza

Juan Ponce de Léon

Juan Rodríguez Cabrillo

Junípero José Serra

Lorenzo de Zavala

Mariano Guadalupe Vallejo

Octaviano Larrazolo

Pedro Menéndez de Avilés

JUAN RODRIGUEZ CABRILLO

BY JOHN BANKSTON

Printing 2 3 4 5 6 7 8 9

Library of Congress Cataloging-in-Publication Data

Bankston, John, 1974-
Juan Rodriguez Cabrillo / by John Bankston.
p. cm. — (Latinos in American history)
Summary: Describes the life of Juan Rodríguez Cabrillo, a sixteenth-century Spanish soldier and explorer who participated in the conquest of Cuba, spent time in the service of Cortes, and undertook explorations which eventually resulted in settlements in southern California.
Includes bibliographical references and index.
ISBN 1-58415-199-4 (lib. bdg.)
1. Cabríllo, Juan Rodríguez, d. 1543—Juvenile literature. 2. Explorers—America—Biography—Juvenile literature. 3. Explorers—Spain—Biography—Juvenile literature. 4. America—Discovery and exploration—Spanish—Juvenile literature. 5. California—Description and travel—Juvenile literature. 6. California—History—To 1846—Juvenile literature. [1. Cabrillo, Juan Rodríguez, d. 1543. 2. Explorers. 3. America—Discovery and exploration—Spanish. 4. California—History—To 1846.] I. Title. II. Series.
E125.C12 B36 2003
970.01'6'092—dc21

2002153057

ABOUT THE AUTHOR: Born in Boston, Massachussetts, John Bankston began publishing articles in newspapers and magazines while still a teenager. Since then, he has written over two hundred articles, and contributed chapters to books such as *Crimes of Passion*, and *Death Row 2000*, which have been sold in bookstores across the world. He has written numerous biographies for young adults, including *Mandy Moore* and *Alexander Fleming and the Story of Penicillin* (Mitchell Lane). He currently lives in Portland, Oregon.

PHOTO CREDITS: Cover: Nancy Walton/National Park Service; p. 6 Hulton/Archive; p. 10 Bettmann/Corbis; p. 13 Archivo Iconografico, S.A./Corbis; p. 14 Bettmann/Corbis; p. 16 Bettmann/Corbis; p. 19 Archivo Iconografico, S.A./Corbis; p. 21 Bettmann/Corbis; p. 22 Hulton/Archive; p. 28 Hulton/Archive; p. 30 Nancy Walton/National Park Service; p. 32 Nancy Walton/National Park Service; p. 34 Robert Holmes/Corbis; p. 38 Nancy Walton/National Park Service

PUBLISHER'S NOTE: This story is based on the author's extensive research, which he believes to be accurate. Documentation of this research can be found on page 46.

The spelling of the names in this book follow the generally accepted usage of modern day. The spelling of Spanish names in English has evolved over time with no consistency. Many names have been anglicized and no longer use the accent marks or any Spanish grammar. Others have retained the Spanish grammar. Hence, we refer to Hernando De Soto as "De Soto," but Francisco Vásquez de Coronado as "Coronado." There are other variances as well. Some sources might spell Vásquez as Vazquez. For the most part, we have adapted the more widely recognized spellings.

CONTENTS

Brutal and unpredictable, Hernán Cortés's conquests required a strong army. He promised them adventure and all the riches the New World had to offer. As a talented young crossbowman serving Cortés, Juan Rodríguez hoped to find both and make his ambitions a reality.

SNEAK ATTACK!

It was raining when they came.

The Spanish conquistador Hernán Cortés led his tiny army of less than 300 men through the wet darkness. Though most were seasoned soldiers, they were badly outnumbered by the forces of his opponent and fellow Spaniard, Panfilo Narváez. Narváez commanded more than 1,000 men and had superior equipment including cannons.

But Narváez was overconfident on this May evening in 1520. The sudden storm was just a delay. Once it ended he would attack Cortés. He anticipated an easy victory. In the meantime, he and his men sought shelter from the heavy rain in their camp near Veracruz, Mexico. As Cortés crept closer, most of Narváez's men were sleeping. This was a mistake.

The roots of this conflict went back more than a year and a half. The governor of Cuba, Diego Velázquez, was interested in conquering Mexico and seizing its vast riches for Spain. To lead his expedition of conquest, Velázquez had two men in mind: Cortés and Narváez. But the two men did not get along, and Cortés owned a stronger taste for conquest.

In November 1518, Cortés rounded up 500 men, packed them onto 11 small sailing vessels and left for Mexico. Velázquez was furious. He ordered Narváez to pursue the renegade Cortés and bring him back to Cuba in chains. Narváez, a longtime rival of Cortés, was more than happy to oblige.

Cortés drove deep into Mexico and achieved a foothold in the vast Aztec capital of Tenochtitlán (today's Mexico City). It was the richest city in the New World. When he heard that Narváez had landed on Mexico's east coast, he left some of his men in Tenochtitlán. Then he hurried back to the coast to deal with Narváez.

If the two forces had met on an open battlefield, Narváez almost certainly would have won because of his superior numbers and greater armament. But Cortés had no intention of doing anything like that. So he led his men silently toward Narváez' camp beneath the shroud of rain and darkness. They quickly disarmed the few sentries and sliced the saddles off the horses. Because of the rain, the cannons had been plugged with wax to keep the powder dry. They were useless.

The battle was over almost before it began. Hernán Cortés had won another victory. During the brief assault, Narváez lost an eye and ended the night in chains. He would spend many more months in his shackles before Cortés released him.

Following this success, Cortés made an offer to the men who'd been with Narváez. Go back to Tenochtitlán with him and enjoy all the wealth the New World had to offer. It wasn't a hard choice. Very few of the men owed any allegiance to Narváez. Almost all of them had come to the New World to get rich. So nearly every man accepted the offer.

One of them was a young crossbowman. He'd arrived in the New World with nothing, working as a helper to the son of a wealthy merchant, then as a page, or young servant, for Narváez. Neither position had provided him with much money. So Cortés's offer was very appealing.

Already he'd proven himself a skilled soldier in Cuban battles. He's also spent three years learning the craft of shipbuilding and had become skilled in the fundamentals of navigation. All of these talents would be put to use, first under Cortés's command, and then on his own. Not only would the young crossbowman go on to discover California, before he died he would be one of the wealthiest men in North America.

His name was Juan Rodríguez Cabrillo. While he never became very famous, he was an important Latino explorer whose initial journey along the western coast of North America provided guidance for future explorations. These helped to expand Spanish territory and eventually led to the first settlements in California.■

The expeditions of Panfilo de Narváez were extremely violent. He gave little thought to slaughtering unarmed natives. Witnessing Narváez's actions influenced the way Juan later treated tribes when he became a commander.

IMMIGRANT DREAMS

No one knows for certain when or where Juan Rodríguez was born. Indeed, some people even believe that he wasn't born in Spain at all. They think that he was born in Portugal but wound up serving for the Spanish.

One theory is that he was a poor boy who was orphaned at an early age. In the shadows of an enormous church in Seville, Spain, street children like him begged for change from the parishioners who came and went along its steep stone steps. These children lived a difficult and dangerous life. But with no one to take care of them, they had few choices. Like many street kids, they did what they could to survive. But unlike nearly all the others, Juan Rodríguez was lucky.

Instead of leading a life of poverty, Juan was spotted by Alonso Sánchez de Ortega. Ortega was a rich merchant who lived in Seville, one of Spain's major port cities. The man invited the poor boy to live with him and his family. In the 1500s, members of Spain's upper class would occasionally take in less fortunate children.

Ortega had become involved with trade to the New World, sending ships loaded with cargo to newly discovered islands like Jamaica and Hispaniola (the home of today's Haiti and the Dominican Republic). Only a short time before, in 1492, Christopher Columbus had discovered the New World while searching for a trade route to Asia. As a result, Spanish merchants and the royal family discovered a new source for what seemed like unending wealth.

The territory also kept soldiers busy, as many native tribes fought back against the Spanish they saw as invaders. Often the soldiers—called conquistadors—killed natives who hadn't even fought. So along with cargo and merchants, the ships carried arms and soldiers.

Panfilo de Narváez was one of their commanders. Narváez was an hidalgo—a man who worked for the royal family. His job was to do whatever they told him to do. In 1510, they wanted him to assemble a force of men and sail for the New World. He'd be reporting to Diego Velázquez, who would soon become governor of Cuba.

Although historian Gonzalo Valdez would later describe Narváez as an "hidalgo who came to these parts with only a sword and a cape searching for adventure," he actually left Spain with provisions, horses, soldiers and soldiers-in-training.

Juan Rodríguez must have been one of them.

Although his exact birth date is unknown, Juan Rodríguez was probably ten to twelve years old when he joined Narváez's trip to the New World. He was one of many "Juan Rodríguezes" sailing to North America in the 16th century. In fact, because "Juan Rodríguez" was a name as common in Spanish as "John Smith" is in English, he would add "Cabrillo" to it when he became a wealthy man.

Juan Rodríguez didn't just have a common name, he had a common dream. In the early 1500s, the area around Seville contributed one-third of the people who came to the New World. Like many immigrants, they sought adventure, opportunity and riches. Juan Rodríguez would eventually possess all of these.

He was joined in his passage to North America by Diego Sánchez de Ortega, the son of the merchant who'd taken him in. Diego would eventually become Juan's close friend and brother-in-law. But when Juan left Spain in 1510, the former street urchin was probably little more than Diego's assistant.

In late 1510, Narváez landed in Jamaica. Over the next several years, Juan and the other young boys who made the trip would be trained in everything from hand-to-hand combat to how to use the harquebus (an early version of the musket) and the crossbow. He was

Although Christopher Columbus's 1492 discovery of the New World was an accident, it led to a rush of Spanish explorers seeking adventure in the 1500s.

especially talented with the crossbow—a useful skill during a time period when the harquebus was a crude weapon. Though its exploding gunpowder created noise and smoke that frightened the Indians, it often jammed or took too long to load. Crossbows could fire their arrows much more efficiently, and Juan Rodríguez had good aim.

In the Spanish army, a talented soldier could rise quickly in the ranks regardless of his family background. This was especially true in the New World. Becoming a military leader also meant access to great riches.

However, before Juan would enjoy the spoils of war, he would first witness its many horrors.

Christopher Columbus had discovered Cuba during his first voyage in 1492. Two years later the explorer would return to the island. By the

Like many priests in the New World, Bartolomé de las Casas (shown here) provided a written record of the Spanish explorations and conquests. His account of Narváez's bloodshed provided one of the best records of the explorer's brutality.

early 1500s, Spanish leaders were convinced that the island was brimming with gold. So around the same time that Narváez and young Juan Rodríguez arrived in Jamaica, Diego Velázquez landed on the beaches of Cuba with some 300 men. He planned to survey and conquer as much of the island as possible, taking its wealth for Spain—and keeping enough for himself to live in luxury.

He and his men constructed a crude log fort and began their preparations for battle. When the natives fought more fiercely that he'd expected, he called for back-up. Narváez brought with him some thirty skilled crossbowmen and numerous Jamaicans they'd enslaved. Cabrillo probably came along as a page to Narváez.

In the early part of 1511, Narváez led his men on a long march through the interior of Cuba. One evening they stopped at a village called Caonao. The natives greeted the tired and hungry Spaniards with water and food. While the Spanish enjoyed their hospitality, the natives looked over the horses. They'd heard of such animals, but had never seen them. The natives stood peacefully near the animals.

As soon as the Spanish had finished eating, one of them raised his sword. That was a signal for the rest of the men to move in, also with their weapons raised. Before the natives could respond, they were attacked. It became a fierce and brutal slaughter. Some 2,000 Indian men, women and children were slain. So were many of their domestic animals.

If young Juan was there, witnessing such savagery might have convinced the pre-teen that this was the way things were done in the New World—these were the rules. Natives could be befriended, but killing them required no reason or motivation.

Every Spanish expedition was accompanied by at least one Catholic priest. On this trek, that priest was Bartolomé de las Casas, who reported, "I saw such terrible cruelties done there as I had never seen before nor thought to see."

Las Casas was so horrified by it all that he took the unusual step of quitting right then and there. His last words to Narváez as he passed over the bloodstained earth were "You and your men can go to the devil!"

But Narváez did not go to the devil. A few years later, he went to Mexico instead. And Juan Rodríguez would go with him.■

Montezuma II believed Spanish explorer Hernán Cortés was a god. Cortés would use his resemblance to Quetzalcoatl to gain the Aztec leader's trust.

CHAPTER 3

A GOD AMONG MEN

Hernán Cortés was a god. At least, that's what many of the Aztecs believed—especially their emperor, Montezuma II. It's easy to see why. The Aztecs worshipped a god named Quetzalcoatl, who they believed was light-skinned and bearded. Just like Cortés. Maybe he wasn't Quetzalcoatl, but the Aztecs were sure he carried messages from their god.

Messages which demanded obedience.

Of course, Hernán Cortés was not a god. He was a conquistador—Spanish for conqueror. He was just one of hundreds who'd come to the New World during the early 1500s dreaming of wealth.

Like Juan Rodríguez and many of the young men from Spain, Cortés dreamed of adventure and seizing land for Spain, land which would make him rich. But unlike many of his peers who arrived on North American shores in the 16th century, Cortés made his dreams come true.

He arrived in the New World as a 19-year-old in 1504, accompanying a band of Spanish merchants who landed on the island of Hispaniola. The island, which was eventually divided into modern-day Haiti and the Dominican Republic, gave Cortés a starting point as he developed a small plot of land and bided his time. He was good at making friends with powerful men like Diego Velázquez. When Velázquez went to Cuba, Cortés joined him. Not as a soldier, but as a treasurer.

Hernán Cortés's talent for counting gold would soon come in handy.

In Cuba, Cortés continued to acquire and develop land while also serving as mayor of Santiago. But the conquistador was growing restless. Eventually he encountered soldiers fresh from Mexico, who described a region filled with untapped wealth. Cortés knew his ambitions lay across the warm waters of the Gulf of Mexico. He also knew the trip could be very dangerous. Along with the stories of wealth came descriptions of the natives' fighting abilities. These were far superior to anything he'd encountered among the islands of the Caribbean.

Juan Rodríguez was also listening to stories of adventure in Mexico.

By now, he had had several years of training with the crossbow. He was comfortable in the saddle of a horse. He'd also added shipbuilding and navigating to his list of skills. So by the time he was in his late teens, Juan Rodríguez was like Cortés: bored and dreaming of adventure.

But while Juan Rodríguez was still a poor teenager, Cortés had grown successful in Cuba. Still, he was willing to risk it all on a Mexican gamble. He gained the essential support of Velázquez, who appointed Cortés as captain-general of the trip. Cortés sold his property—everything he owned, in fact—to finance his expedition. He organized a navy of nearly a dozen ships and hired more than five hundred men. They were veterans of campaigns in Cuba, Hispaniola and even Mexico.

By November of 1518, Cortés was ready to sail. Unfortunately, the more men he got for the mission, the more nervous Velázquez became. He worried that Cortés would take the wealth for himself, or go around him directly to the royals in Spain. Velázquez decided to officially remove Cortés from command.

But Cortés learned of the governor's change of heart in advance before he could be officially removed. So he had his men board the ships in secret, under the cover of night. At first light on the morning of November 18th, Cortés went through Santiago's butcher shops, taking every ounce of meat for him and his men. They sailed out of Santiago before Velázquez could stop them.

As ruler of the Aztecs, Montezuma II led his people into terrible battles with local tribes, and used many thousands of them for human sacrifices. Because of this many of the people surrounding Aztec territory were willing to join Cortés in his battle against them.

The ships landed on the island of Cozumel off the east coast of Mexico's Yucatán Peninsula. Then Cortés made his way slowly along Yucatán's northern coast. Along the way, he gained gifts of food and the promise of peace. He also was given a beautiful teenage slave named Malintzin. She spoke Nahuatl, the language of the Aztecs, which would soon make her especially useful to him. From her and the other natives he encountered, Cortés learned where the real wealth of Mexico was.

It was with the Aztecs, and it was well guarded.

Even as Cortés was preparing to fulfill his dreams of conquest and riches, back in Cuba Governor Velázquez was fuming. The governor wrote a letter to the King of Spain, asking the ruler to recognize Velázquez's authority over both Cortés and any riches or land the conquistador seized.

Then, even as he waited for a response, the governor prepared for battle. He organized nineteen ships, loading them with provisions and weapons that included twenty cannons outfitted with enormous amounts of gunpowder. He recruited more than 1,000 solders, eighty horsemen and ninety crossbowmen.

Juan Rodríguez was one of them.

While these preparations were going on, Cortés marched further along the Yucatán coast, heading towards Aztec territory. When he finally reached a place that he considered suitable to establish a base, Cortés took an unusual step.

Besides being a skilled military leader, Cortés was also familiar with the law. He knew from his experiences as mayor of Santiago how to establish a town. So he created the community of La Villa Rica de Vera Cruz. A few of his men formed a ruling council and elected Cortés mayor. As the head of his own town in Mexico, he was now answerable only to Spain. As the governor of Cuba, Velázquez no longer had authority over him.

Soon the conquistador met his first Aztecs. They came bearing gifts from Montezuma, their leader. Their language was translated by Malintzin. When the warriors requested one of their metal helmets, Cortés gladly gave it.

A few days later, one of the Aztecs chiefs returned, carrying the helmet. It was filled with gold.

Malintzin had even more surprising news. The men were calling Cortés "teule." She told him what that meant. They thought he was a god.

She also told him the best way to use the information.

In the fall of 1519, Cortés was ready to march toward the Aztec capital, carrying information about their city, their defenses, and their weapons.

Before they left Veracruz, Cortés wanted to show his men how serious he was about conquering the Aztecs.

He ordered the burning of their own ships.

Now there was no turning back.■

Cortés refused to imagine surrender or retreat. He wanted to make sure his men didn't consider turning back once the battle started. He guaranteed their loyalty by ordering them to torch their ships.

The Aztecs believed "tonally" kept the world moving. Tonally supposedly collected in the heart of a person who was afraid. The tribe created fear by ripping still-beating hearts from their human sacrifices.

CORTES'S REVENGE

As he traveled from Veracruz to the Aztec city of Tenochtitlán, Cortés found tribespeople who were more than willing to help him. Everywhere he encountered natives who hated the Aztecs—for good reason. The Aztecs practiced human sacrifice and often used their neighbors for the ritual.

In addition, many of the tribes that were ruled by the Aztecs had been defeated in battle. They had no allegiance to Montezuma other than fear. They would follow anyone who threatened his harsh rule.

By November of 1519, Cortés had reached Tenochtitlán. It was a mass of pristine white buildings at the center of Lake Texcoco. Low-lying bridges called causeways connected the city to the mainland. Instead of warriors waiting for battle, the Spanish found the city open to them and were able to march over the bridges and along its wide streets unharmed. Probably the most modern city in all of North America, the Aztec home was a thing of beauty and wonder. But it was also a place of enormous brutality.

Although the Aztecs welcomed the Spanish, feeding and lodging them, the soldiers grew increasingly distressed. Often they watched as the Aztecs practiced their religion. It was religion that demanded ritual sacrifice on an enormous scale.

Every year some 20,000 people were killed. Many were captured warriors who were brought to the top of one of Tenochtitlán's pyramids and strapped to a flat stone altar. One of the Aztec high priests would ceremonially remove the victim's still-beating heart. The rest of the body was tossed down the steps.

It was not discarded, however. The corpses's legs and arms were harvested, and provided a meal for Aztec royalty or for the men who had captured them. Emperor Montezuma was said to enjoy cooked thighs covered in chili peppers.

The Spanish learned that the ritual sacrifice was practiced because of a belief in "tonally" or animating spirit. This was found in the blood and collected in the heart whenever a person was frightened. It's hard to imagine anything scarier than facing a ritual Aztec sacrifice, so this ceremony provided an abundance of "tonally." The energy was needed because the Aztecs believed without it, everything on earth would freeze. Only the sacrifices would keep things moving.

Having witnessed these ceremonies, some of the Spanish were ready to move as well. They began to wonder if their own beating hearts were about to be used to "keep the world moving."

Instead of waiting for the slaughter, Cortés took Malintzin and a few of his soldiers into the throne room of Montezuma's mighty palace. There Montezuma gave the conquistador another surprise. The Aztec emperor explained that he didn't want to fight or sacrifice the Spanish. He was certain they were messengers from the gods. In fact, he knew Cortés was fulfilling an ancient Aztec prophecy—that their god would some day come down from the heavens and take their land.

That sounded pretty good to Cortés. Using Malintzan as his translator, he explained he needed to take the emperor prisoner. Montezuma agreed to be put under house arrest. Everything was going exactly as Cortés planned.

Then he learned about Panfilo Narváez. Now the conquistador faced challenges on two fronts—at the Aztec city and back at the city he'd created.

He left a small group of soldiers at Tenochtitlán under the command of Pedro de Alvarado. He ordered them to guard Montezuma and keep the peace. Then with about 250 of his best soldiers, Cortés quickly made the return trek of nearly 200 miles back to Veracruz.

After surprising and quickly defeating the overconfident Narváez, Cortés had the reinforcements he needed. They included Juan Rodríguez.

In Tenochtitlán, Cortés would need every man he could get. During his absence, Alvarado had enraged the Aztecs by killing hundreds of them during a feast day. By the time Cortés and his soldiers entered the city, the Aztecs were agitated. Before he realized it, he and his soldiers were trapped in the heart of the city. All around them, furious Aztec warriors prepared for battle. They cut numerous trenches across the causeways. At some point, Montezuma was killed, either by arrows fired by his own men or by the Spanish.

Cortés ordered his men to gather their gold and tried to work out a plan. He had them build a portable bridge, which would be put over the gaps in the causeways as they advanced and then removed after their crossing. It might have worked—if not for greed.

At midnight on June 30, 1520, the Spanish tried to escape from what had now become a trap along one of the two-mile causeways that linked the city to the mainland. But the causeway was so narrow that only a few men could march side by side.

Weighed down by hundreds of pounds of gold, the men made poor soldiers. When the Aztecs attacked, the outnumbered Spanish were slaughtered. Hundreds were killed or captured. Some even endured their worst fear: sacrifice. The horrible retreat became immortalized as Noche Triste, or "sad night."

Juan Rodríguez was one of the lucky ones. He managed to escape. And Cortés's forces may have been decimated, but they were not defeated. They retreated into the mountains to prepare a counterattack. Once there, they had a stroke of luck. Another ship sent by Velázquez arrived. Its men had intended to assist the already defeated Narváez. But instead of fighting Cortés they joined him.

Buoyed by the arrival of more men, Cortés decided to construct a fleet of small ships under the protection of friendly Indians. It was obvious to him that he had to have control of the lakes surrounding Tenochtitlán in order to control the city itself.

And here Juan Rodríguez's skills as a ship builder proved vitally important.

A fellow soldier described Juan from that time. "During the conquest of Mexico, after the Aztecs expelled the Spanish from the city," recalled Francisco López, "during those days this witness saw him carry out orders both as a soldier and as one charged with preparing material and fittings for the [small ships] they were building in order to re-conquer the city by way of the lake of Mexico. This Juan Rodríguez was a man of the sea and he understood that sort of work."

Even though the ships would be only about 40 feet long, Cortés wasn't taking any chances. He wanted them to be so powerful that the Aztecs couldn't possibly defeat them. Finding enough wood for the thick hulls and heavy decks in the highlands where he had taken refuge wasn't a problem. But he also needed many of the same materials that were used in building ships capable of crossing oceans. Materials such as towing line and cables, sails and rigging, iron fittings and bolts. And above all, cannons.

None of these were available locally.

But they were readily available among the ruins of the ships he had destroyed back in Veracruz before he had set out the first time. So Cortés sent some men back to Veracruz to salvage everything he could from the hulks of those ships. More than 1,000 native tribesmen, still hoping for the overthrow of the Aztecs, eagerly volunteered to carry the material.

Then the Spanish set to work to build the ships. They were provided with masts and sails. In addition, there were benches and oars so they could be rowed. There was enough room for several crossbowmen and men firing harquebuses. No Aztec canoe could stand up to them.

One of the most important things they needed was resin from the trees, which was one of the ingredients used to create pitch which would be painted along the exterior of the ships to make them waterproof. The resin was poured into large cauldrons which were heated. Unfortunately, in Mexico there were no cattle which could contribute the beef tallow, or fat, which was part of the process of making pitch.

While some researchers doubt the story, historian Gonzalo Oviedo reported Juan Rodríguez's solution: "They had no oil or tallow for tarring the boats. As a substitute they used human fat, from the hostile Indians they had killed, of whom there were a great number."

The ships were completed in safety. Then they were carefully dismantled. With thousands of Indians carrying the parts and more thousands protecting them from attack, Cortés led a long procession back into Aztec territory. As they approached Lake Texcoco, Cortés ordered a canal to be dug. The ships were reassembled and one by one, floated into the lake.

The battle began in late April of 1521. The sturdy little ships were at the head of a fleet of canoes filled with the Indian allies of the Spanish. Aided by a breeze that sprang up just in time and gave them added momentum and power, the little ships smashed through the Aztec canoes that tried to stop them. That enabled the Spanish to seize control of the causeways leading into the city. This blockade cut off Tenochtitlán from receiving any supplies or reinforcements. Then the ships began bombarding the city with their cannons.

There could be no doubt about the outcome. This time the Spanish succeeded. The only sadness came from the defenders. In several months of fighting, historians estimate that as many as 100,000 Aztecs perished. The city of Tenochtitlán was turned into a pile of smoking rubble. Those who survived the Spanish onslaught were struck by a much tinier weapon—disease germs. Because the natives had never encountered smallpox they had no immunity to it, and many died as a result. Countless others died of starvation.

By August of 1521, Cortés was the undisputed leader of Mexico.

Juan Rodríguez "came out wounded," as one of his sons would later recall, but he healed quickly. For his ingenuity and his bravery, Juan Rodríguez was about to get his first taste of the spoils of war.■

Using ships constructed by Juan Rodríguez and under the command of Hernán Cortés, the Spanish attacked the Aztec city of Tenochtitlán. The battle lasted for months, and over 100,000 tribesmen perished before Cortés's victory.

NEW MONEY

After conquering some of the fiercest warriors in the New World, the Spanish celebrated with food and wine.

However, when the party ended, the men who served under Hernán Cortés's command faced a difficult reality. Once Spain took its portion, and Cortés his, there was little Aztec gold left over. For his contribution to the campaign, Juan Rodríguez received enough gold to buy a horse. Although this was a rare possession for a New World soldier, he was hardly rich.

The riches would arrive with more conquests.

To the south, warring tribes had cut off supplies and made travel for the Spanish risky. By now Juan was a combat-hardened officer. When he enlisted in the campaign of Francisco de Orozco he knew his rank would assure him a greater share of the spoils than he'd gotten under Cortés.

If he lived long enough.

The Mixtecs had earned a fearsome reputation and when Juan Rodríguez joined the battle in late 1521 he knew anything could happen. However when they reached the Mixtec stronghold of Itzquintepec, Orozco's forces surrounded the main army and cut the

Poised and prepared for battle, this model of Juan Rodríguez Cabrillo about to draw his sword stands in the exhibit room of the Cabrillo National Monument in San Diego, California.

natives off from their supplies. Facing starvation, the Mixtecs surrendered.

Juan Rodríguez received his first real taste of what the New World could offer. For sparkling beneath the surface of the streams which ran along the perimeter of Itzquintepec was gold. The land itself was rich. For officers like Juan Rodríguez, this potential wealth was best exploited using a Spanish system known as the "encomiendas."

Encomiendas were offered as a reward to officers and other soldiers who fought well in the New World campaigns. These men became "encomenderos," entitled to oversee large sections of land which was worked by the natives. These natives would then pay a tribute, a portion of all the gold they mined or food they grew.

In return, the encomenderos were supposed to introduce the natives to the Christian religion and to protect them. But it isn't surprising that the encomenderos were far more interested in the benefits than the obligations.

The encomienda system practically guaranteed an extremely comfortable life—for the encomenderos. It was close to slavery for the natives who fell under it. So it may have been surprising that Juan Rodríguez turned down the offer of an encomienda near Itzquintepec. It wasn't because he was opposed to the system. It was just that the former beggar child was certain greater riches were just around the corner.

He was right.

Soon Juan transferred his allegiance to Pedro de Alvarado, even though the man's brutality became legend in a time known for brutality. His treatment of the Aztecs in Cortés's absence had nearly gotten everyone killed.

But despite his mistakes, early in 1522 he was about to embark on another campaign. Juan Rodríguez joined Alvarado's march as commander of a large group of crossbowmen. First they established Ciudad Oaxaca. Then the force continued south to Tututepec. Owning both superior forces and a fearsome reputation, the Spanish didn't even have to fight. The Tututepec people surrendered. Afterwards, Alvarado's plunder began in earnest as he demanded large payments of gold and held the natives' religious leaders for ransom. Even Alvarado's horse was given a gift—a pair of golden stirrups that were designed for the animal's saddle.

But still greater riches lay further south, in the country we now know as Guatemala.

Because of the need to deal with various minor incursions, 1523 was almost over before Alvarado embarked on his Guatemalan campaign. He led an army which numbered three hundred soldiers and

After three months at sea, Juan Rodríguez Cabrillo and his party arrived in San Diego on September 28, 1542.

over 20,000 tribesmen. They were supported by 130 skilled crossbowmen under the command of Juan Rodríguez.

It was lovely country, filled with peaceful towns, well-cultivated fields and plenty of water from clear, clean streams.

As had been the case in Mexico, an ancient civilization stood in the Spaniards' way. This time it was the Quiché Indians. Their capital city of Utatlán compared favorably with Tenochtitlán and had been in existence for hundreds of years.

The rulers had a desperate plan. They would lure the invaders into the city, then light it on fire and kill them. The Quiché would lose their city, but at least they could rebuild.

But Alvarado became suspicious and withdrew before the trap could be sprung. He soon captured the Quiché leaders and either hanged them or burned them at the stake. Then he destroyed the city and enslaved its population.

On August 12, 1524, the city of Santiago de Guatemala was founded in what had been an Indian cornfield. It was designated as the country's first capital and Juan Rodríguez was central to its planning. The city had about 100 founders, and each man signed his name in a book that still exists. Juan Rodríguez was among the first to put down his signature.

So by the summer of 1524, young Juan Rodríguez was thoroughly enjoying the spoils of war. He took a native woman as his bride. Although her name is unknown, she would bear Juan several children. While very little is known about them, some records suggest that the daughters from this marriage in turn married conquistadors.

Juan Rodríguez would continue to assist Alvarado in his campaigns through Guatemala and the modern-day countries of El Salvador, Honduras and Nicaragua. These battles would consume much of the next dozen years.

He was well-rewarded for his efforts. He became an encomendero several times over, which in the untapped wealth of Guatemala meant far more riches to Juan than he would have had in any previous opportunity.

In fact, Juan would soon become one of the richest men in the New World.■

Peering out over San Diego Bay, this statue of Juan Rodríguez Cabrillo is part of the Cabrillo National Monument in San Diego, California which was created in 1913.

CHAPTER 6

THE WEALTHY SHIPBUILDER

The veterans of the Spanish campaign were not an attractive lot. "They looked like they have escaped from hell, they are so badly maimed," one young woman reported. "Some have lost a foot, others a hand, others have no ears, others have one eye; others half a face. The handsomest have been scarred once or twice or three times."

Almost certainly Juan Rodríguez was just as scarred. By the early 1530s he probably looked old for his age, but he'd chosen wisely in selecting his encomiendas. The several properties paying him tribute produced both food and gold.

He also formed a lucrative partnership with Diego Sánchez de Ortega. When the pair had arrived in the New World years earlier, Juan had been little more than a servant to the son of the man who had taken him in. Now the two were equals.

As a wealthy landowner, Juan felt he deserved a new wife, one of Spanish heritage. Rich with new money, Juan Rodríguez Cabrillo left for Spain. The woman he sought was familiar—she was Beatriz Sánchez de Ortega, Diego's sister. They were married in 1632 and

Juan brought her to his now very large estate on the outskirts of Santiago.

The rest of the 1530s saw Juan's wealth increase but his ambitions were not over. During his explorations along the western coast of Guatemala, he had noticed thick stands of hardwood trees. So he began to develop a shipbuilding business and his talents were quickly recognized by Guatemala's governor—Pedro de Alvarado. His former commander was interested in further exploration.

At that time no one realized the vastness of the South Sea, as the Pacific Ocean was known at that time. Many people, including Alvarado, believed that the rich Asian markets weren't too far away. So he went back to Spain to get a license to conquer any islands he could discover in the South Sea. Alvarado wanted Juan to build a fleet of ships that could open up this trade.

In addition, explorers believed that somewhere to the north was a passage called the Strait of Anian that ran between the Atlantic and Pacific Oceans. Though no such passage existed, the Spanish didn't know it at the time. Whoever discovered such a passage would become wealthy.

The quest to share in some of these riches would eventually cost both Alvarado and Juan Cabrillo their lives.

But in August of 1541, it was still a dream when Juan Cabrillo wrote that, "It has been perhaps six years since he [Alvarado] went to Spain and at the time he ordered that I should build him an armada while he was in Spain and so I built it."

Although he makes the job sound easy, the task of constructing ships suitable for such an exploration was long and hard. He faced much the same situation that he had faced 15 years earlier during the re-conquest of Tenochtitlán. The hulls, decks and masts of the ships could be produced locally, using the trees that he'd discovered.

But nearly all of the specialized equipment he needed—everything from iron bolts to heavy anchors that weighed hundreds of pounds—could only be imported all the way from Spain, which involved voyages of several months in duration. The equipment was put ashore on the Atlantic side of the central American isthmus. He used thousands of Indians for the bone-crushing labor of hauling the materials over mountains and steaming jungles. No one knows how many of them perished.

Eventually the job was done. All told, Cabrillo had been responsible for building 13 ships. They were manned by about 1,000 sailors and arrived in Navidad, Mexico, about halfway up the Mexican coast on Christmas Day 1540.

The expedition had already attracted the interest of Antonio de Mendoza, the viceroy of Mexico, who bought into the expedition. The plan that Mendoza worked out with Alvarado was two-fold. The larger group of ships, under the command of Ruy López de Villalobos, would head west into the Pacific. The others, with Cabrillo at their head, would sail north. Hopefully they would find the Strait of Anian.

But Alvarado never got a chance to take advantage of the ships that had been built for him. During a native uprising in 1541, a warhorse rolled over the hapless commander. The accident broke a number of Alvarado's bones. He survived for only a few days. That didn't stop Mendoza from continuing the planned expeditions.

Cabrillo's efforts were interrupted by a natural disaster of cataclysmic proportions. In the early morning of September 11, 1541, Santiago was struck by an earthquake. Most of the flimsy dwellings of the city collapsed, and many people who survived the initial shock were killed by mudslides.

Afterwards, Juan Cabrillo toured the awful devastation. He felt moved to provide a written account of what had occurred. His pamphlet, "Relación del Espantable," was the first non-religious piece of journalism written in the New World. Juan Cabrillo's straightforward account of the aftermath of an earthquake provided valuable information to future residents of South America.

While the quake and other matters consumed his attention for several months, Cabrillo eventually returned to his tiny fleet.

On June 27, 1542 Cabrillo sailed out of the port of Navidad. He would never return.■

Commanding the San Salvador, *along with two other ships, Juan Rodríguez Cabrillo sailed out into unknown waters, hoping for New World wealth. Discovery and death awaited.*

CALIFORNIA!

Cabrillo was aboard the *San Salvador*, the largest of the three ships under his command. According to the best estimates, the vessel was about 100 feet long, 25 feet wide, drew 10 feet of water and weighed about 200 tons. It had a crew of more than 60 men in addition to 25 soldiers and at least one priest. It was armed with several cannons, which fired stone balls of about the same diameter as a compact disc. The *San Salvador* was accompanied by the *Victoria* and the much smaller *San Miguel.*

Meals were based on whatever fish they could catch, along with beans, hard biscuits, salted meat and other items prepared by the cabin boys. Everything was washed down with wine. Officers ate better than the crew members, and many of them brought their own private stocks of food. Scurvy—a disease caused by the lack of vitamin C—was a constant worry.

They sailed up the coast of Mexico, then crossed to Baja California and edged steadily northward along the western coast of the peninsula. On August 20, they reached the furthest point that previous expeditions had reached. Now they were truly headed into the unknown.

A month later they sailed into what is now Ensenada, some 30 miles south of today's California-Mexico border. Then on September

28—103 days after leaving Navidad—the little fleet dropped anchor in what Cabrillo termed "a very good enclosed port." It was the feast day of San Miguel, so Cabrillo gave the bay the name of the saint. Though the bay would be renamed San Diego sixty years later during another expedition, it is Cabrillo's most famous discovery.

They stayed there for several days, then headed north again. Cabrillo visited several islands along the coast, such as San Clemente and Santa Catalina. He explored other areas and often gave them place names according to something he noticed. Thus Santa Monica was Bahia de la Fumos (Bay of Smokes) due to the haze from many Indian campfires. Ventura was El Pueblo de las Canoas (the town of the canoes). And a site west of Santa Barbara was christened El Pueblo de las Sardinas (the town of the sardines) because of the large quantity of the tiny fish that the inhabitants gave them.

At every place he went ashore, Juan Cabrillo took a sword, drove its point into the ground and declared the land to be Spanish territory. His men would then slice down trees and mark the area.

He also read what was called the *el requerimiento* ("the requirement"). It was a document that informed the Indians that they had just become Spanish subjects and must accept the Christian religion. Even though Cabrillo read it in both Spanish and Latin, the natives had no idea what he was talking about.

So it wasn't surprising that they found these actions odd. They could not know that Cabrillo's actions heralded future explorations and eventual conquest by the Spanish.

Accounts of Cabrillo's treatment of the native tribes are universally positive. Having witnessed so much brutality, Cabrillo did not repeat the actions of men like Cortés and Alvarado. He traded with the natives and did everything he could to make sure his men treated them fairly.

One example came soon after their arrival in San Diego. The natives slightly wounded three men with arrows. Cabrillo's response was to capture two boys, then release them unharmed and loaded down with presents.

As they cruised along the coast by modern-day Oxnard, Ventura and Santa Barbara, they found the region well-populated by peaceful Indians. The natives would often paddle their canoes in company with the ships, and the two groups frequently exchanged presents. It is likely that these Indians also provided fresh food. They certainly provided no threat to Cabrillo.

But as the three ships neared Point Conception, what had been a smooth voyage changed. At that point the coast bends almost ninety degrees, from east-west to north-south. There was no longer any protection from the fierce northern winds, especially as winter grew closer. It was nearly a month and several tries before the ships were able to pass north of Point Conception.

After that they made good progress and sailed at least as far north as Monterey. They might actually have reached Point Reyes, well beyond the entrance to the San Francisco Bay. But by now, storms were whipping across the ships, sweeping cargo from the *Victoria* and damaging the *San Miguel*. With few other options, Cabrillo decided to sail south again and seek shelter.

The exhausted men, their vessels barely seaworthy, landed on the island of San Miguel in late November and began repairing their ships. It is the outermost of the Channel Islands that lie about 25 miles off the coast south of Santa Barbara. Here the natives were more warlike, and Cabrillo and his men were ill-prepared for the conflict. "All the time the armada was in the Isla Capitana (the original name that the Spanish gave the island), the Indians never stopped fighting us," a sailor named Francisco de Vargas reported.

Death arrived a month later, as one of Cabrillo's captains sailed ashore seeking fresh water. The natives attacked in droves. Outnumbered, the captain called for reinforcements. Juan Cabrillo was not one to let his men fight the battles alone. He quickly tried to rescue them. He boarded a small boat and raced to the shoreline.

"As he began to jump out of the boat," Vargas remembered, "one foot struck a rocky ledge, and he splintered a shinbone." Despite suffering excruciating pain, Juan Cabrillo refused to leave until all of his men were safely on board the boat. Only then did he retreat.

In a different time or a different place the broken bone would have been a minor injury. But on the isolated island, with only crude medical attention, the broken leg quickly became infected. Cabrillo knew he was dying.

"He called captain [Bartolomé] Ferrer and gave him command as captain general of the armada, by the authority of the royal commission that he held," reported sailor Lázaro de Cárdenas.

On January 3, 1543 Juan Rodríguez Cabrillo died.

Following Cabrillo's orders, Ferrer resumed the expedition's northward course. Because of the unreliability of the primitive navigational instruments used at that time, no one knows how far north Ferrer was able to sail. Some historians believe that he may have reached the mouth of Oregon's Rogue River, some 30 miles beyond today's California border.

But after constantly fighting storms and with dwindling supplies, Ferrer had little choice but to return. The ships were separated by strong winds and high seas. With the aid of favorable winds, they were reunited at Cedros Island off the Baja California coast. The three ships returned to Navidad on April 14, 1543.

The expedition was considered a failure at the time. Neither Cabrillo nor Ferrer had been able to find the passage connecting the oceans. That wasn't surprising, because such a passage did not exist. Nor had they found any gold. And virtually all the place names that Cabrillo bestowed on the places he discovered would be replaced by future explorers. It is ironic that San Miguel, the name he bestowed on his greatest discovery—San Diego Bay—would eventually become the name of the place where he died.

Yet because of his efforts, the Spanish learned much about Southern California—enough to begin the centuries-long process of colonizing the region, erecting settlements and missions in the state.

He had come to the New World a poor child, and become a rich man. He had discovered California.

The Cabrillo National Monument was created in San Diego in 1913 to recognize his work. His statue overlooks the bay that he entered more than 400 years ago.■

CHRONOLOGY

1498-1500	born at unknown location
1500s	begins begging outside cathedral in Seville; is taken in by Alonso Sánchez de Ortega
1510	sets sail for New World
1519	joins mission to battle renegade conquistador Hernán Cortés
1520	joins Cortés's army as crossbowman after Narváez's defeat
1521	aids in conquest of Aztecs; joins Francisco de Orozco in subduing Mixtecs in Oaxaca
1522	assists in plundering the wealth of Tututepec
1523	marches on Guatemala with Pedro de Alvarado
1524	marries native woman; registers as citizen of Guatemala and helps build capital city of Santiago
1532	marries Beatriz Sánchez de Ortega in Spain
1534	takes a ship on trading voyage to Peru
1536	begins shipbuilding business in Guatemala
1541	records effects of devastating earthquake in Santiago, Guatemala
1542	leaves on voyage of exploration to California
1543	dies of injuries on January 3

TIMELINE IN HISTORY

1492 seeking new trade route to Asia, Christopher Columbus discovers West Indies

1498 Portuguese navigator Vasco da Gama discovers sea route to India by sailing around the southern tip of Africa

1500 Juan de la Cosa publishes first map of the New World

1502 Montezuma II becomes emperor of Aztec nation in Mexico

1513 Vasco Núñez de Balboa crosses Isthmus of Panama and discovers Pacific Ocean

1513 Juan Ponce de León discovers Florida

1519 Hernán Cortés enters Aztec capital city of Tenochtitlán and is received by Aztec ruler Montezuma II

1522 Ferdinand Magellan reaches Philippine Islands on his expedition around the world but is killed by natives; his crew completes the voyage

1526 Esteban Gómez establishes but soon abandons settlement on the Savannah River (present-day Georgia)

1527 Rome attacked by troops of Charles V, King of Spain, and Pope is imprisoned

1527 Álvar Núñez Cabeza de Vaca begins ill-fated expedition to Florida under command of Panfilo Narváez; Cabeza de Vaca is one of only four survivors

1530 Don Antonio de Mendoza becomes Mexico's first viceroy

1531 Francisco Pizarro begins conquest of Peru

1534 Jacques Cartier begins exploring the St. Lawrence River for France

1536 King Henry VIII orders second wife Anne Boleyn beheaded

1538 geographer Gerardus Mercator uses "America" to refer to the entire New World for the first time

1540 Francisco Vásquez de Coronado sets off on expedition from Mexico that eventually passes through Arizona, New Mexico, Texas, Oklahoma and Kansas

1541 Hernando de Soto becomes first European to cross Mississippi River

1543 Nicolaus Copernicus publishes theory that sun is center of the universe and the earth revolves around it

1551 Real y Pontificia Universidad de Mexico becomes first university on the North American continent

1555 tobacco brought from America to Spain for the first time

1565 Pedro Menéndez de Avilés establishes St. Augustine, Florida, which becomes oldest US city.

1607 Jamestown colony founded

FOR FURTHER READING

For Young Adults:

Lemke, Nancy. Cabrillo: *First European Explorer of the California Coast.* San Luis Obispo, CA: EZ Nature Books, 1991.

Lovelace, Maud Hart. *What Cabrillo Found.* New York: Thomas Y. Crowell Company, 1958.

Podell, Janet and Steven Anzouin. *Old Worlds to New.* New York: The H.H. Wilson Company, 1993.

Smith, Carter (editor). *The Conquest of the West.* Brookfield, CT: Millbrook Press, 1992.

Smith, Carter (editor). *Exploring the Frontier.* Brookfield, CT: Millbrook Press, 1992.

Works Consulted:

Bolton, Herbert. *The Spanish Borderlands*. New Haven, CT: The Yale University Press, 1921.

Kelsey, Harry. *Juan Rodríguez Cabrillo*. Huntington, CA: Huntington Library Press, 1998.

Lavender, David. *DeSoto, Coronado, Cabrillo: Explorers of the Northern Mystery*. Washington, D.C.: Division of Publications, National Park Service, 1992.

Mee, Charles L. Jr. "That Fateful Moment When Two Civilizations Came Face to Face." *Smithsonian Magazine* Oct 1992: 56-69.

Nauman, James D., ed. *An Account of the Voyage of Juan Rodriguez Cabrillo*. Cabrillo National Monument Foundation Staff, 1999.

Wagner, Henry R. *Juan Rodriguez Cabrillo*. Lawton R. Kennedy Publishers (private printing), 1999.

Juan Rodriguez Cabrillo
http://www.mms.gov/omm/pacific/kids/Cabrillo.htm

San Diego Biographies: Juan Rodriguez Cabrillo
http://www.sandiegohistory.org/bio/cabrillo/cabrillo.htm

Juan Rodriguez Cabrillo
http://www.socalhistory.org/Biographies/cabrillo.htm

The History of San Diego: The Explorers
http://www.sandiegohistory.org/books/pourade/explorers/explorers.htm

National Park Service: Cabrillo National Monument
http://www.nps.gov/cabr/juan.html

Aztec Hamlet: The Tragedy of Moctezuma II
http://www.mexconnect.com/mex_/history/jtuck/jtmoctezuma2.html

GLOSSARY

armada (ar-MAH-dah) - a large group of moving ships or people

cataclysmic (kat-uh-KLIZ-mik) - disastrous

conquistador (con-KEES-tah-door) - Spanish for conqueror; one of the men who used violence to take over portions of native territory

crossbow (CROSS-boe) - bow mounted on a wooden stock which fired darts with tremendous force

encomendero (en-koam-en-DARE-oh) - owner of an encomienda

encomienda (en-koam-ee-EN-duh) - large estate in the New World in which the land and the natives are under the control of an encomendero and must provide a portion of their earnings to him

hapless (HAP-less) – unfortunate, having bad luck

harquebus (HAWR-kuh-bus) - heavy long gun that preceded the musket

hidalgo (ee-DOLL-go) - member of minor nobility in Spain who works for the king

isthmus (ISS-muss) - a narrow strip of land that lies between two larger bodies of land

league (LEEG) - distance of approximately three miles

New World – North, South, and Central America (The "Old World" was whatever was known to Europeans in the 15th century)

renegade (REN-uh-gade) - one who changes his allegiance, often suddenly and with treachery

scurvy (SKUR-vee) - disease caused by a lack of vitamin C in the diet (found mainly in citrus fruits like oranges and lemons) which causes bleeding beneath the skin and weakness; often fatal to sailors on long voyages

viceroy (VISE-uh-roy) - Spanish governor who ruled as direct representative of the king of Spain

INDEX